BEGINNERJAZZ
SOLOINGFORVIOLIN

The beginner's guide to jazz improvisation for violin & concert pitch instruments

BUSTERBIRCH

FUNDAMENTALCHANGES

Beginner Jazz Soloing for Violin

The beginner's guide to jazz improvisation for violin & concert pitch instruments

ISBN: 978-1-78933-179-0

Published by **www.fundamental-changes.com**

Copyright © 2020 Buster Birch

The moral right of this author has been asserted.

All rights reserved. No part of this publication may be reproduced, stored in a retrieval system, or transmitted in any form or by any means, without the prior permission in writing from the publisher.

The publisher is not responsible for websites (or their content) that are not owned by the publisher.

Over 10,000 fans on Facebook: **FundamentalChangesInGuitar**

Instagram: **FundamentalChanges**

Cover Image Copyright: Shutterstock: Alenavlad

Violin examples played by Liz Norton

Contents

Introduction 5

Get the Audio 6

Chapter One – Step One: Playing *by ear* 7

Chapter Two – Step Two: The Minor Pentatonic Scale 11

Chapter Three – Step Three: Scale Patterns 13

Chapter Four – Step Four: Rhythmic Phrasing 18

Chapter Five – Step Five: Creating Melodies 23

Chapter Six – Step Six: Question and Answer Phrasing 27

Chapter Seven – Now Improvise Your Own Solos 30

Chapter Eight – Jazz Articulation 36

Chapter Nine – Composition 45

Chapter Ten – Taking it Further 50

About the Author

Buster Birch is an award-winning jazz educator from London, UK. He has been a professorial member of the jazz faculty at Trinity Laban Conservatoire of music for seven years where he taught improvisation, musicianship, jazz repertoire and jazz history classes. He has been a visiting lecturer at The Royal Academy of Music, The Guildhall School of Music & Drama, and Middlesex University.

He is co-director of the UK's longest running jazz summer school **www.theoriginalukjazzsummerschool.com**, a week-long residential course hosted at The Royal Welsh College of Music & Drama for singers and all instrumentalists of all ages and experience levels. He runs two regular jazz workshops for adult learners **www.saturdayjazzworkshop.co.uk** and **www.tonbridgejazzworkshop.co.uk**

He is a co-founder and the course leader for BYMT Jazz School (**www.bymt.co.uk**) which runs regular jazz improvisation classes for junior and secondary school students at the county music centre. In 2017 BYMT Jazz School won the prestigious Will Michael Diploma Award for Jazz Education, a national award recognising "outstanding commitment to jazz education" and "acknowledging the work of those field practitioners who are actually delivering jazz education and in many cases helping to combat the widespread jazz phobia among classroom music teachers and instrumental tutors."

Buster Birch is also a busy freelance jazz drummer who has worked with many of the UK's finest jazz musicians. He has an honours degree in music from the University of London and a post-graduate diploma in jazz performance from the Guildhall School of Music and Drama. He also studied at the Drummers Collective in New York City and privately with Jim Chapin and Joe Morello (of The Dave Brubeck Quartet).

He has performed at virtually every major concert hall and jazz club in London, as well as major international festivals, toured in over thirty countries and recorded over thirty CDs. He has been a member of three world music groups with whom he recorded and toured extensively. He has played for world-class orchestras, including The Royal Philharmonic Orchestra, and deputised on West End shows.

He created his own critically acclaimed show **www.busterplaysbuster.com** which features the Buster Birch Jazz Quartet playing live and in sync to the screening of Buster Keaton feature-length silent movies, for which he has arranged and scored over 4hrs of music.

In addition to his freelance work, he is a member of the following bands: ARQ (The Alison Rayner Quintet) – winners of the UK Parliamentary Award for "Best Jazz Ensemble 2018", The Jo Fooks Quartet, Heads South, The London Jazz Trio, The Sue Rivers Quintet and The Halstead Jazz Club Big Band.

For more information, please see **www.busterbirch.co.uk**

Introduction

This is not a *how to play the violin* book. It is a *how to play music* book.

The concepts used throughout this book are universal and apply to any instrument, but the exercises have been tailored to fit within a suitable range for each specific instrument. There are certain details and references, especially in the chapter on jazz articulation, which are specific to each different instrument.

It is assumed that you have a basic working knowledge of your instrument and fingerings are not provided.

Not all, but most violin players have a *classical* background of learning and are not self-taught. If so, then they have probably spent a lot of time learning how to play their instrument and learning to read music. Their performing experience might be limited to taking music exams and playing in school ensembles or local amateur orchestras. There is nothing wrong with any of that, but they may not have spent much time exploring improvisation through jamming with friends or learning tunes by ear from recordings – things that rock and pop guitarists, bass players and drummers tend to do a lot.

This *classical training* might not have taught them a great deal about harmony, as they won't have had much need for that knowledge. All of the notes are written out for them and they don't need to create their own parts. The theory they learned may be rudimental and focused on the rules of notation rather than the practical details of how music works, and this theory might have been forced upon them as a requirement to pass an exam. As a result, they could have learned it by rote without having a thorough understanding of how it fits into the bigger picture.

This particular experience of learning to play music can result in an underdeveloped ear and a debilitating fear of playing *wrong* notes, which can overwhelm them. It can even prevent them from ever attempting to improvise. Over time, this fear and reluctance to improvise becomes more entrenched. It can reach the point where the thought of improvising anything is an unbearable leap into the dark.

If any of this sounds familiar then do not worry, this is the book for you! Anyone can learn to improvise. Improvising requires an additional set of skills, all of which can be learned and, with practice, mastered.

As a teacher, I learned that the most important thing of all is the process. A clear pathway and small steps make all the difference.

All of the exercises and concepts presented in this book have been tried and tested in my regular jazz workshops with adult learners and school children. Over the years they have been refined, and I have developed a method that breaks down the process into six manageable steps. As you overcome each small challenge, your confidence grows and you get closer to your goal of improvising freely. This method avoids the terrifying leap into the unknown and does not overwhelm you with too much theory.

Each step in this method focuses on one particular element and provides practical exercises to help you develop the skills required. Once you complete all six steps, you will be fully equipped to improvise a solo and, most importantly, that last step will be a small one, instead of a great big leap.

I have seen the results this method can produce and look forward to sharing them with you. I hope you find this book helpful. There is a lot of material to get through, so take your time and work at your own pace.

Get the Audio

The audio files for this book are available to download for free from **www.fundamental-changes.com.** The link is in the top right-hand corner. Simply select this book title from the drop-down menu and follow the instructions to get the audio.

We recommend that you download the files directly to your computer, not to your tablet, and extract them there before adding them to your media library. You can then put them on your tablet, iPod or burn them to CD. On the download page there is a help PDF and we also provide technical support via the contact form.

www.fundamental-changes.com

Instagram: FundamentalChanges

Chapter One – Step One: Playing *by Ear*

The essential starting point when learning to improvise is playing by ear. Playing by ear means that instead of reading the music off the page, you play the notes that you hear in your head. Playing by ear uses a different part of your brain from reading and lets you develop a deep connection with the music. Some musicians initially find it harder to play by ear, but like any skill this is developed with regular practice (called ear training), and I'm yet to find anyone who hasn't been able to develop this valuable skill.

Most young children can play by ear well if it is taught in a fun, entertaining way. Many adult learners, however, who have spent a lifetime playing classical music are often terrified of playing by ear. Yet, they are often much better at it than they could ever imagine. The key to success is learning in small steps and allowing your ears time to develop. Very few people can play the examples in this book perfectly on the first attempt, so relax and allow yourself to make mistakes.

In this chapter we are going to learn to improvise (invent melodies) by ear. Starting with just one pitch, we will add one note in each exercise until we are playing a common five-note scale called The Minor Pentatonic scale – and important sound in Jazz, Blues and Rock music. We'll use the same minor pentatonic scale for the whole of this book and you will learn how to improvise solos and compose your own tunes with it.

The following exercises are based on a common practice referred to as *call and response*. You will be told which notes to play, but have to work out the rhythm and sequence of notes by ear.

You'll need to refer to the audio files now, so make sure you have downloaded them from **www.fundamental-changes.com**

One Note Improvising

For the first two exercises you will only use one note (F). You can play it in any octave.

The *Response*

On audio Example 1a you will hear a four-beat count in, then a two-bar phrase (this is the *call*) followed by two bars rest. You should play during the two bars rest. Try to copy the *call* exactly and keep in time with the rhythm section. Your phrase is the *response*. Repeat this for each of the eight different phrases on the track.

The *Call*

Now use audio Example 1b to practice improvising your own two-bar phrases with the same note (F). Play similar phrases to those you heard in the previous example. Keep the same structure by playing for two bars, then resting for two bars. You are now playing the *call* and the rest bars are space for the imaginary *response*. Start playing straight after the four-beat count in.

When improvising your *calls* try to imagine the whole phrase in your head before you play it. Use each two bars rest to think about your next phrase. *Hearing* the phrase before you play it will really help your timing.

Two Note Improvising

Now you are going to add another note (Ab) which is a minor third up from the F.

The *Response*

Using audio Example 1c, listen to each two-bar *call* and then play the *response*. Try to copy the *call* exactly and keep in time with the track.

Try to keep the sound of both notes in your head throughout the whole exercise. Doing this will help you identify the different pitches as you hear them. The backing track is in the key of F, so when you play F it should feel like *home*.

The *Call*

Use audio Example 1b again to improvise some *calls* with these two notes. Keep the same structure by playing for two bars, then resting for two bars. Try to *hear* your next phrase before you play it. Start playing immediately after the four-beat count in.

Three Note Improvising

Now you are going to add another note (Eb) which is a tone down from F. With these three notes (Eb, F, Ab) you can create some very familiar sounding melodies. You would be surprised at how many blues, pop and folk melodies are written with just these three notes!

The *Response*

Using audio Example 1d, listen to each two-bar *call* on the track, then play the same phrase as a *response* in the two bars rest. It is a little more challenging now. Try to hear the different *quality* of each note so that you can recognise them individually.

Use the F as your marker point. F should still feel like *home* with the Ab and Eb sounding like they are either side of it.

The *Call*

Now use audio Example 1b again to improvise some *calls* with these three notes. Play similar phrases to those you heard in Example 1d. Again, keep the structure by playing for two bars, then resting for two bars and try to *hear* your next phrase before you play it. Start playing immediately after the four-beat count in.

Four Note Improvising

Now you are going to add another note (C) which is a perfect fifth up from F. The C stands out from the other three notes because it is much higher, but it also helps to confirm the original note (F) as *home*. Play the F and C on your instrument now. Listen to how they sound together. The interval of a perfect fifth is quite distinctive and is one often heard in many styles of music.

Recognising the sound of different intervals is very useful when playing by ear. Sing the first two notes of *Twinkle, Twinkle, Little Star* out loud and you will be singing a perfect fifth. Using the first two notes of a well-known tune gives you an easy way to recognise and remember a particular interval.

Using four notes is much more challenging, so don't worry if you make some mistakes. It will take time to develop these skills, but practising like this will help your improvising. You don't have to use all four notes in every phrase. You just have more choice now.

The *Response*

Using audio Example 1e, listen to each two-bar phrase, then play the same phrase as a *response* in the two bars rest. By now, you should be fairly familiar with the first three notes, so this extra note (C) should stick out. It will probably take a few attempts before you get all eight phrases correctly, but that is fine and to be expected.

The *Call*

Now use audio Example 1b again to improvise some *calls* with these four notes. Remember, you don't have to use all four notes in every phrase. To start with, try some different two or three note combinations.

Five Note Improvising

Now you are going to add the final note (Bb) which is perfect fourth up from F. Sing the first two notes of *Here Comes The Bride* out loud and you will be singing a perfect fourth. Play the F and Bb on your instrument now. Now play the F and C. Hear the different quality or *flavour* of these two intervals. Try to remember this difference as you complete the last two exercises.

The *Response*

Using audio Example 1f, listen to each two-bar phrase, then play the same phrase as a *response* in the two bars rest. Listen out for the Bb and the C and try to identify them individually. If you find this too hard, don't worry, just go back and do some more practice on the previous exercises. When you can confidently identify the first four notes, this last one will be much easier to spot.

The *Call*

Lastly, use audio Example 1b to improvise some *calls* with these five notes. You don't have to use all five notes in every phrase. Start with some different three-note combinations and then add the other notes as you go along.

When improvising, always avoid *wiggling the fingers* and seeing what comes out! Keep it simple. Simple phrases can sound great if played with confidence and *hearing* the phrase before you play it will give you that confidence. A great rule to follow is…

Hear What You Play And Play What You Hear

You don't have to completely master everything in Chapter One before moving on – these are warm-up exercises and something you can come back to. But, if you can play all eight phrases from Example 1f correctly and have improvised your own melodies using all five notes, you are doing really well and have laid some great foundations for the rest of the book.

Chapter Two – Step Two: The Minor Pentatonic Scale

If you take the five notes you have learned in Chapter One and rearrange them into the following sequence, it makes the F Minor Pentatonic scale.

Example 2a:

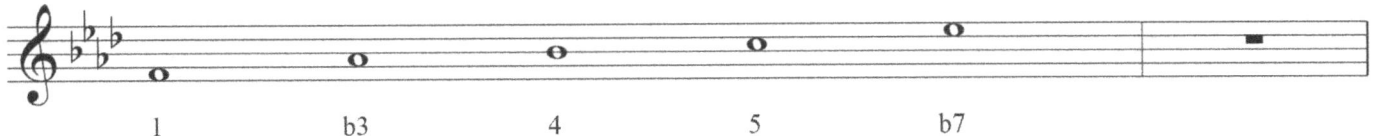

A pentatonic scale is any scale that has five (Greek: *penta*) notes in it, so there are many different types of pentatonic scale. However, in practice, most musicians would only ever refer to a *major* or *minor* pentatonic scale. For the purposes of this book we are going to use only the F Minor Pentatonic scale, so you need to commit these five notes to memory.

The minor pentatonic is a great scale to use when creating melodies because it has a well-balanced mix of steps and leaps built in. If you improvise with a standard seven-note scale (like the major scale), you can end up with too much step-wise movement and not much shape to the melody. If you improvise with chord tones (arpeggios), you end up with very angular phrases because you are playing *all leaps*. Using the minor pentatonic scale automatically solves both of these common issues.

An excellent way to remember the notes of any scale is to think of the interval sequence…

The Interval Sequence

When learning a new scale, it is helpful to think about the intervals (the space between the notes). Any scale is just a sequence of intervals, so if you learn the sequence then you can play the scale in any key, you just need to start on a different note.

The interval sequence for F Minor Pentatonic is:

F (minor third) **Ab** (tone) **Bb** (tone) **C** (minor third) **Eb** (tone) **F**

If you want to transpose the minor pentatonic scale to a different key, just play the same interval sequence starting on a different note. For example, Bb Minor Pentatonic is:

Bb (minor third) **Db** (tone) **Eb** (tone) **F** (minor third) **Ab** (tone) **Bb**

Notice that the sequence of intervals is the same for both scales.

The Blues Scale

There is another scale that you may already know, which is very similar to the F Minor Pentatonic scale. If you add a B (#4), then you get the F Blues scale.

Example 2b:

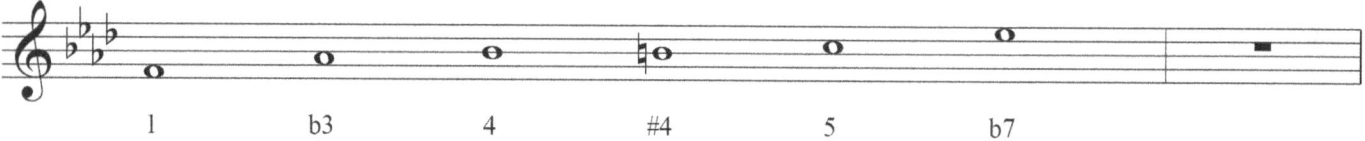

It is worth bearing this in mind because the #4 in a blues scale has no real harmonic function and works as a *passing note*. It is also referred to as a *blue note*. Because the #4 is such an inconsequential note, harmonically speaking, it means that the minor pentatonic and blues scale are interchangeable. There are many other books written about the blues scale and how to use it, so I won't go into more detail here. Suffice to say that where you can use one, you can use the other.

Chapter Three – Step Three: Scale Patterns

Scales are a great resource and something that all musicians should practise regularly. However, the traditional method of practising scales, up and down from root to root, is not much help when it comes to improvising. The problem is, you are only learning the notes in one particular sequence. Repeated practice then makes this one sequence a fixed habit.

When you are improvising, you need to be comfortable moving from any note in the scale to any other note in the scale. If you have only practised the notes in one particular sequence, you are really limiting yourself. Practising scale patterns will free you from this habit and help to *unlock* your scales.

There are so many different scale patterns, starting on every note of the scale, it would be impossible to include them all in this book. What I have provided here are some examples to demonstrate the concept. This chapter contains eight scale patterns, plus another four which are combinations of the first eight patterns, giving you twelve different scale patterns to practice. You should also make up some of your own.

Because of the mixture of leaps and steps in the minor pentatonic scale (as discussed in Chapter Two), these scale patterns include irregular intervals. The resulting combination of leaps and steps can be challenging at first but will be of great benefit later. They require your brain to be fully engaged when practising and that is always a good thing!

Scale Pattern Exercises

For each of the following exercises, start by playing it slowly, without the track. Make sure you understand the sequence of notes (the pattern) in relation to the scale, which is explained before each exercise. Then play along with the track at the slowest tempo. Listen to the track as you play to check your accuracy. When you can play the whole exercise four times without a mistake, move up to the next tempo. There are five tempos for each exercise.

As you practise these exercises, try to think of each note by its number (degree of the scale), rather than its letter. Of course, you need to know what the letters are to play them on your instrument, but thinking in numbers will be beneficial later when you need to play in other keys. The numbers are written under all of the notes to help you.

These examples all use the F Minor key signature, so watch out for the Ab, Bb and Eb!

The first pattern moves up the scale two notes, then back one. It starts on the root.

Example 3a: 60bpm, 90bpm, 120bpm, 150bpm, 180bpm.

The next pattern moves down the scale two notes, then back one. It starts on the root.

Example 3b: 60bpm, 90bpm, 120bpm, 150bpm, 180bpm.

The next pattern moves up the scale skipping a note, then back one. It starts on the third.

Example 3c: 60bpm, 90bpm, 120bpm, 150bpm, 180bpm.

The next pattern moves down the scale skipping a note, then back one. It starts on the fifth.

Example 3d: 60bpm, 90bpm, 120bpm, 150bpm, 180bpm.

The next pattern moves up the scale three notes, then back two. It starts on the root.

Example 3e: 60bpm, 90bpm, 120bpm, 150bpm, 180bpm.

The next pattern moves down the scale three notes, then back two. It starts on the third.

Example 3f: 60bpm, 90bpm, 120bpm, 150bpm, 180bpm.

The next pattern moves up the scale skipping a note, skipping another note, then starts again from the next note of the scale. There are a lot of fourth intervals, which can be unfamiliar. It starts on the root.

Example 3g: 60bpm, 90bpm, 120bpm, 150bpm, 180bpm.

The next pattern moves down the scale skipping a note, skipping another note, then starts again from the next note of the scale. There are a lot of fourth intervals, which can be unfamiliar. It starts on the root.

Example 3h: 60bpm, 90bpm, 120bpm, 150bpm, 180bpm.

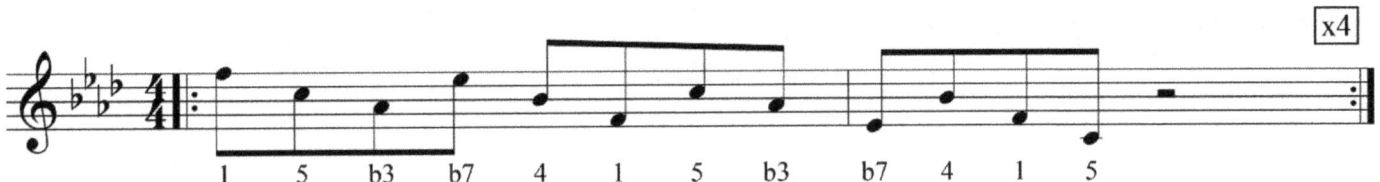

Combining Scale Patterns

The next pattern combines the first bar of Example 3b and the second bar of Example 3a.

Example 3i: 60bpm, 90bpm, 120bpm, 150bpm, 180bpm.

The next pattern combines the first bar of Example 3c and the second bar of Example 3d.

Example 3j: 60bpm, 90bpm, 120bpm, 150bpm, 180bpm.

The next pattern combines the first two beats of Example 3e and the remainder of Example 3f.

Example 3k: 60bpm, 90bpm, 120bpm, 150bpm, 180bpm.

The next pattern combines the first three beats of Example 3h and the remainder of Example 3g.

Example 3l: 60bpm, 90bpm, 120bpm, 150bpm, 180bpm.

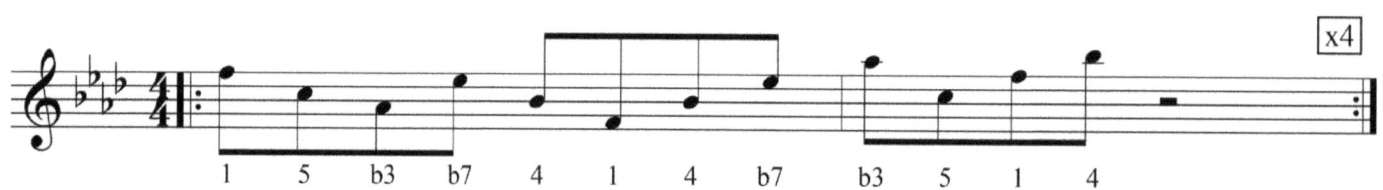

As you can see, the possibilities are endless. Don't forget to make up your own scale patterns and have fun exploring those as well.

The purpose of these exercises is to break the old habit of just playing up and down, root to root. Practising scale patterns will help to *unlock* your scales.

These exercises are written to fall in a comfortable range on your instrument, but you should also practice extending the same patterns over the whole range of your instrument.

Chapter Four – Step Four: Rhythmic Phrasing

By now you should be feeling pretty confident with the F Minor Pentatonic scale. You should know all the notes of the scale in different octaves without having to think too hard about it.

The previous chapter was all about pitch, and this chapter is all about rhythm.

In this chapter you are going to learn some stock rhythmic phrases, which you will use in the next section to create melodies. Memorising these different rhythms will also give you the building blocks for your improvised solos later in the book. When learning a new language, you usually start by learning stock phrases. This method also works well when learning to improvise because it provides you with musical language that you can use right away.

Included here are sixteen different rhythmic phrases for you to learn. As you practise each one, try to hear the whole phrase in your head *before* you play it.

You don't have to memorise all of these before moving on through the book. You could take one phrase and learn it, apply it through the rest of the book, then come back and do the same with the next one. You can also practise the phrases in any order.

But before you start working on the rhythmic phrases, let's take a quick look at *swung quavers*…

Swung Quavers vs Straight Quavers

We sometimes use shortcuts when writing music. There are certain conventions and protocols that have evolved over many years. When sight reading (using notation to perform music that you are not familiar with) it is generally preferable if there is less ink on the page. The less there is to look at, the quicker your brain can process it.

Swung quavers are created when you play the first and last notes of a quaver triplet. Traditionally, this would be written in a compound time signature like 12/8 (Example 4a) or notated as individual triplets in a simple time signature like 4/4 (Example 4b). However, both of those methods use a lot of ink.

One solution is to notate the quavers as straight quavers (Example 4c) but write *swing* or *swung quavers* over the part. This score marking tells the performer to adjust the rhythmic value of the notes and play the second quaver of each beat as if it was the last note of the quaver triplet, which is a *swung* quaver. With a bit of practice, this becomes quite easy to do. Using this method of notation means there is less ink on the page and your brain can process the information much faster.

Example 4a:

Example 4b:

Example 4c:

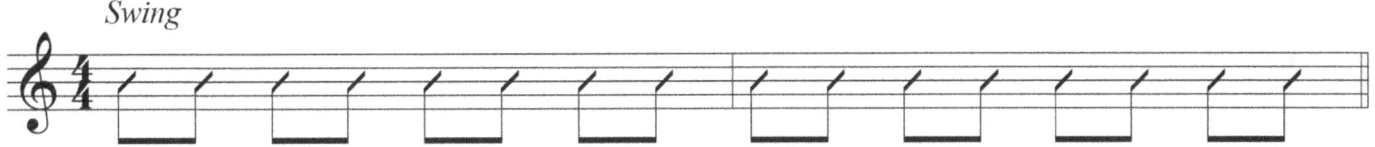

Rhythmic Phrases

For each of the following examples, start by clapping the rhythm. Do this a few times, until you can hear the whole two bars as a complete rhythmic phrase. If there are too many notes to process, try breaking down the phrase into smaller segments. Work on the segments separately, then join them back together.

Of course, hearing the rhythm played for you will make it much easier, but that won't improve your sight reading. So, *before* you listen to the track, see if you can figure it out on your own. Then use the audio file to check your accuracy.

If you can clap it four times correctly with the track, then play it four times on your instrument using only one pitch (F).

The following examples all use *swung* quavers.

Example 4d:

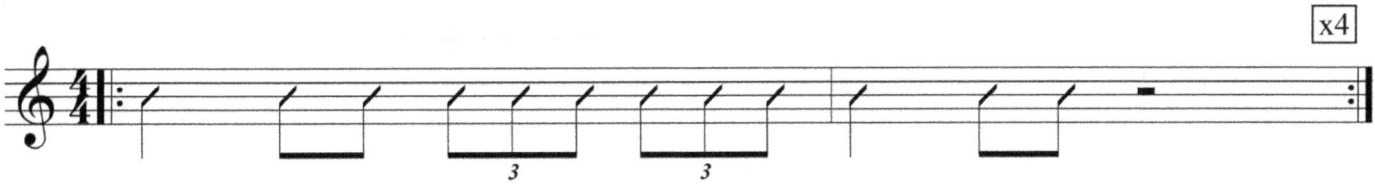

Example 4e:

Example 4f:

Example 4g:

Example 4h:

Example 4i:

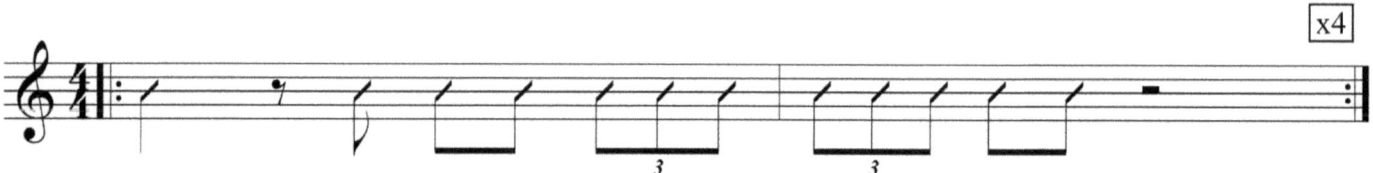

Example 4j:

Example 4k:

The following examples all use *straight* quavers.

Example 4l:

Example 4m:

Example 4n:

Example 4o:

Example 4p:

Example 4q:

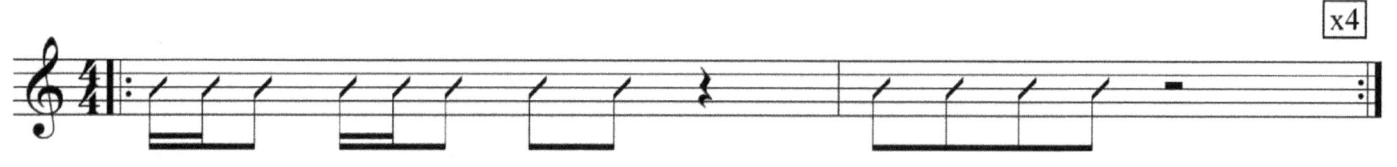

Example 4r:

Example 4s:

Chapter Five – Step Five: Creating Melodies

Now you will combine the scale patterns you learned in chapter three with the rhythmic phrases you learned in chapter four and create some two-bar melodies. Some melodies will sound better than others, but don't concern yourself too much at this stage, these are all just preparatory exercises. Focus on the process and don't worry about the outcome yet. You are developing the skills required to improvise your own great melodies later in the book.

The audio files are provided for you to practise along with. After the count-in, each melody is played four times. If you can play it with the track four times in a row with no mistakes, then move on to the next one.

Applying Rhythmic Phrases to Scale Patterns

For the next few exercises, you will use the same scale pattern and apply different rhythms to that sequence of notes. There isn't space in this book to notate every possible combination. What is provided are a few samples to show you the process. You should work through the rest of the combinations on your own.

As a reminder, go back and play Example 3a a few times. Now go back and clap Example 4d a few times. If you combine that scale pattern with that rhythmic phrase, you create the following melody.

Example 5a:

Keeping the same scale pattern (3a) but applying rhythmic phrase 4e creates the following melody. Clap the rhythm before you play the phrase. Go back and listen to Example 4e if you need to check the rhythm.

Example 5b:

Keeping the same scale pattern (3a) but applying rhythmic phrase 4f creates the following melody.

Example 5c:

Keeping the same scale pattern (3a) but applying rhythmic phrase 4g creates the following melody.

Example 5d:

By now you should be getting the idea of how this process works. Stick with this one scale pattern and work it through the remaining twelve rhythmic phrases, then do it all again with a different scale pattern. This will take some time and is not meant to be done all in one session! Make a list of the various combinations and tick them off as you work through them.

Applying Scale Patterns to Rhythmic Phrases

For the next few exercises, you will use the same rhythm and apply different scale patterns to it. Again, there is not space in this book to notate every possible combination. What is provided here are a few samples to show you the process. You should work through the rest of the combinations on your own.

As a reminder, go back and clap example 4l a few times. Now go back and play example 3e a few times. If you combine that rhythm with that scale pattern you create the following melody.

Example 5e:

Keeping the same rhythm (4l) but applying scale pattern 3f creates the following melody.

Example 5f:

Keeping the same rhythm (4l) but applying scale pattern 3g creates the following melody.

Example 5g:

Keeping the same rhythm (4l) but applying scale pattern 3h creates the following melody.

Example 5h:

By now you should be getting the idea of how this process works. Stick with this one rhythm and work it through the remaining eight scale patterns, then do it all again with a different rhythmic phrase. This will take some time and is not meant to be done all in one session! As before, make a list of the various combinations and tick them off as you work through them.

Painting by Numbers

Combining all twelve of the scale patterns with all sixteen of the rhythmic phrases will produce one hundred and ninety-two different two-bar melodies based on an F Minor Pentatonic scale. If you were to apply this process through all twelve keys, then you would generate two thousand, three hundred and four melodies. That would take some time to work through! Practising everything through all 12 keys is a long-term goal and not something you should obsess too much about. But, it is essential to transpose what you learn, so start with some of the more common keys first.

This *painting by numbers* approach might feel a bit prescriptive for some, but it is really about developing a process. You don't have to complete every example in this book before you start making up your own melodies. Just work on a few of these exercises each day, then spend some time developing your own ideas as well.

Working methodically and thoroughly like this will increase your control over your playing, and that is the goal. These exercises will help you to hear what you play and play what you hear, instead of just wiggling your fingers and seeing what comes out. They will help to clarify your ideas and improve your phrasing, making your solo much more pleasant for the listener.

With regular practice, over time, this will become an automatic process. Pre-programming unconscious *good* habits is how the great improvisers can create such fantastic solos on the spot.

Chapter Six – Step Six: Question and Answer Phrasing

So far, all of the melodies you have created have been two bars long. Now you are going to use a simple and universal technique for creating longer musical phrases. Composers often use this method when writing popular tunes, but you are going to do it in *real* time as you improvise.

You are going to combine two of your previous phrases to make a four-bar musical *sentence*. This sentence will include a *question* phrase and an *answer* phrase. But first, you will work on each phrase separately...

Improvising Question Phrases

When you ask a question, you usually raise your voice at the end of the phrase to indicate that you haven't finished what you are saying. You are going to do the same with musical *question* phrases, but rather than go up in pitch you are simply going to avoid ending your phrase on 1 (F). In music, we refer to this as *unresolved*.

Listen to the sample *question* phrases on audio Example 6a and hear how they sound *unresolved*. All of these melodies avoid landing on F. It is a subtle, but effective way of enticing the listener.

Now use audio Example 6b to practise creating some of your own *question* phrases. Improvise two-bar melodies using the skills you have learned in the previous chapters, just avoid ending your phrase on 1 (F).

The backing track is a vamp on F7 so F Minor Pentatonic will work great over this. Play for two bars and then rest for two bars.

Example 6b:

Improvising Answer Phrases

When you answer a question, you usually lower your voice at the end of the phrase to indicate that you have finished what you are saying. You are going to do the same with musical *answer* phrases, but rather than go down in pitch you are simply going to end your phrase on 1 (F). In music, we refer to this as *resolved*.

Listen to the sample *answer* phrases on audio Example 6c and hear how they sound *resolved*. All of these melodies land on F. It gives a sense of finality to the phrase and subtly tells the listener that musical idea is complete.

Now use audio Example 6b again to practise creating some of your own *answer* phrases. Improvise two-bar melodies using the skills you have learned in the previous chapters, just make sure your phrase ends on 1 (F).

Again, the backing track is a vamp on F7 so F Minor Pentatonic will work great over this. Play for two bars, then rest for two bars.

Example 6b:

The Musical Sentence

Now you are going to put the question and answer phrases together to create a four-bar musical sentence, but there is one important factor you need to address. The sentence must make sense. Your question and answer must sound like they belong together. What you must avoid is a musical equivalent of the following...

"What time is it? There were eleven of us."

This sentence includes a question and answer, but they clearly do not belong together!

The solution is to use the same, or similar, rhythms for both phrases. Repeating clear rhythmic phrases, like those you learned in Chapter Four, will help to tie the musical sentence together.

The following example shows a two-bar question followed by a two-bar answer that belong together. Both phrases start with the same idea and use virtually the same rhythm, with a slightly different ending. The question is unresolved, and the answer is resolved. Including a few *pick up* notes adds interest by extending the melody across the bar line.

Example 6d:

Now use audio Example 6e to practise improvising four-bar musical sentences. Play a two-bar question immediately followed by a two-bar answer and use similar rhythmic phrases to tie them together. Avoid ending your question on 1, but make sure your answer ends on 1.

Example 6e:

Spend as much time as possible on this particular exercise. You are combining all of the different skills you have learned so far. Improvising four-bar question and answer phrases will form the basis for all of your soloing and composing in the rest of the book.

Working on this exercise will program your unconscious mind with good habits. The pace, phrasing and rhythm of your solos will improve, and you will gain control over your playing.

Using the Musical Sentence to Avoid Getting Lost

Practising musical sentences will help you think and hear in four-bar phrases, which is the default phrase length for virtually all styles of music. Most compositions are constructed using four-bar phrases, so if you are thinking like this while improvising, you are more likely to keep track with the structure of the tune.

Thinking in four-bar phrases, as opposed to counting every bar, is the equivalent of zooming out, giving you a better overview of the piece. Batch processing like this enables musicians to memorise whole tunes more efficiently and avoid getting lost when improvising.

If we take something like a standard thirty-two bar song form (often described as AABA), we can see that each section of the music is eight bars long. Instead of counting all those bars it is much easier to think...

Two sentences = A section

Two sentences = A section

Two sentences = B section

Two sentences = A section

Or if we apply the same thinking to a twelve-bar blues then...

Three sentences = 12 bar blues

All twelve-bar blues tunes are built around three sentences, musically and lyrically. The structure is always four plus four plus four, not six plus six or any other derivative, so it makes sense to think this way when improvising over it.

Playing over one-chord vamps is another scenario where thinking like this can be helpful. It may seem easy to improvise over a section of music where the harmony doesn't change, but it is also very easy to get lost with so little on the landscape to orientate you. Thinking in four-bar phrases is a great way to zoom out and keep track of your place in the music when the harmony is static.

Chapter Seven – Now Improvise Your Own Solos

Having worked through all the previous exercises, you should be feeling confident about improvising four-bar question and answer phrases using the F Minor Pentatonic scale, starting on any note of the scale. You should also be hearing the rhythm and shape of the phrases in your head before you play them. This is the key to successful soloing.

Musicians from different genres often use the minor pentatonic scale when improvising. In this chapter, you will practise soloing over backing tracks and learn how to use the minor pentatonic in different musical settings.

Some of these styles may sound unfamiliar to you, so take your time and listen to the track a few times without soloing. Make sure you can follow the notation with the audio track and understand the structure of the music *before* you improvise over it.

When practising improvising don't be tempted to wail away or wiggle the fingers and see what comes out. Stick to playing the question and answer phrases you have learned. Stay focused on the process and don't worry too much about the outcome yet. The goal is to program good habits and develop control over your improvising. Always try to...

Hear what you play and play what you hear.

Soloing on a Bossa Nova

Bossa Nova music evolved in Brazil in the late 1950s but became a worldwide phenomenon thanks to an album by Stan Getz and Joao Gilberto called *Getz/Gilberto*. It won four Grammys in 1965 and brought international attention to this music, setting off the Bossa Nova craze which was to follow.

This exercise uses a one-chord vamp on Fm7. The F Minor Pentatonic scale works well over this chord because all four of the chord tones are in the scale. The only note in the scale that is not a chord tone is the 4th (11th) which also sounds great on a minor chord.

Example 7a:

You can also use F Minor Pentatonic over Fmi6, Fmi9, Fmi11 or Fmi13.

The Bossa Nova rhythm uses straight quavers, so the stock rhythmic phrases you learned in the second half of Chapter Four will be useful now.

Improvise four-bar question and answer phrases over audio Example 7b. To start with, play for four bars, then rest for four bars. Once you can do this comfortably, try playing every four bars.

There are three different versions of this audio track at 90bpm, 120bpm and 150bpm. Start with the slowest and work your way up.

Example 7b:

Soloing on a Jazz Swing Feel

Jazz has existed for over 100 years. Throughout this time it has evolved and is continuing to evolve today. So many different styles of jazz exist, that are so wildly different, it can be confusing for anyone new to this music, and difficult to appreciate the connections which span generations. But one unifying factor that connects all styles of jazz is the improvised solo, which is the ultimate expression of artistic freedom.

Jazz terminology can be confusing because the same words can have different meanings. In jazz, the term *swing* can refer to the style of music played by large and small ensembles in the 1930s, made popular by artists such as Louis Armstrong and Benny Goodman, but it can also refer to a particular rhythmic feel which has been used in many different styles of jazz throughout the decades (see *swung quavers vs straight quavers* in Chapter Four).

This exercise uses a two-chord vamp alternating between Fm7 and Ebm7, and the F Minor Pentatonic scale works well over both of these chords. The Fm7 chord we have already covered. Playing the F Minor Pentatonic scale over the Ebm7 chord creates the intervals 9, 11, 5, 13 and 1, all of which fit with the harmony.

Example 7c:

Listen to the different sound of each chord and use the chord sequence to keep your place in the music. Using one scale to play a melodic phrase over different chords can sound very effective as the harmony shifts underneath it.

This example uses swung quavers, so the stock rhythmic phrases you learned in the first half of Chapter Four will be useful now.

Improvise four-bar question and answer phrases over audio Example 7d. To start with, play for four bars, then rest for four bars. Once you can do this comfortably, try playing every four bars.

There are three different versions of this audio track at 90bpm, 120bpm and 150bpm. Start with the slowest and work your way up.

Example 7d:

Soloing on a Pop Groove

This exercise uses a I-V-vi-IV chord progression, which is one of the most common vamps found in modern popular music. Dozens of classic pop hits are based on this simple four-chord sequence.

The chords in this sequence are all diatonic to the key of Ab Major, so you could improvise using the Ab Major scale, but the F Minor Pentatonic scale also works because it is derived from the *relative minor* scale. There are no notes in the scale that clash with any of the chords in the sequence, so you are free to use this one scale over all of the chords. Each note of the scale works with each chord as follows.

Example 7e:

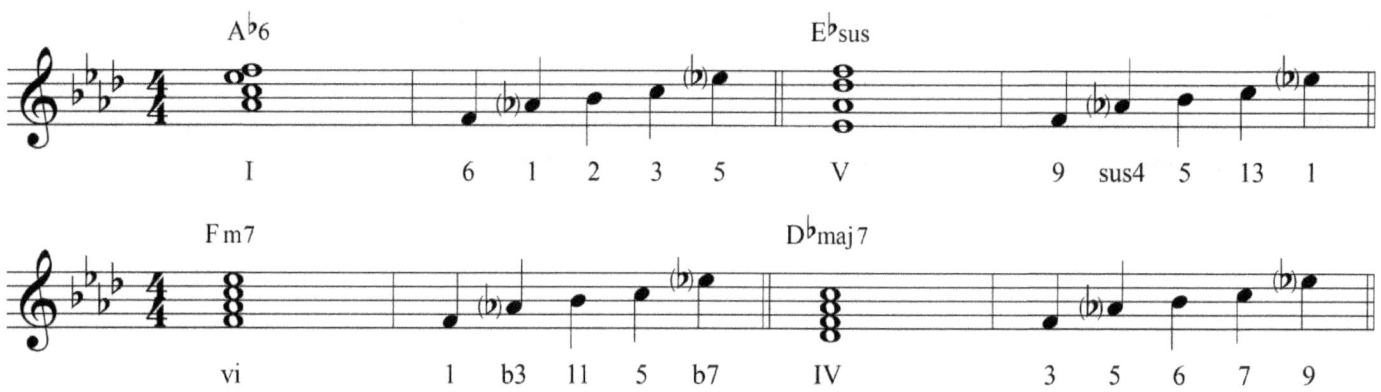

Because you are improvising over the relative major key signature, finishing your *answer* phrase on an F will not sound quite as resolved as it did before. Try using Ab for your resolution and hear the difference.

The Pop beat uses straight quavers, so the stock rhythmic phrases you learned in the second half of Chapter Four will be useful now.

Improvise four-bar question and answer phrases over audio Example 7f. To start with, play for four bars, then rest for four bars. Once you can do this comfortably, try playing every four bars.

There are three different versions of this audio track at 90bpm, 105bpm and 120bpm. Start with the slowest and work your way up.

Example 7f:

Soloing on a Minor Blues

A minor blues is similar to a regular twelve-bar blues, but as the name suggests, is in a minor key. Using a minor chord for the tonic chord (I) has a profound effect on the feel of the music and creates a darker mood.

Mr PC and *Equinox* are two great jazz tunes composed and recorded by John Coltrane that are based on a minor blues.

There are only three chords in this twelve-bar sequence and the F Minor Pentatonic scale works well over all of them, as follows.

Example 7g:

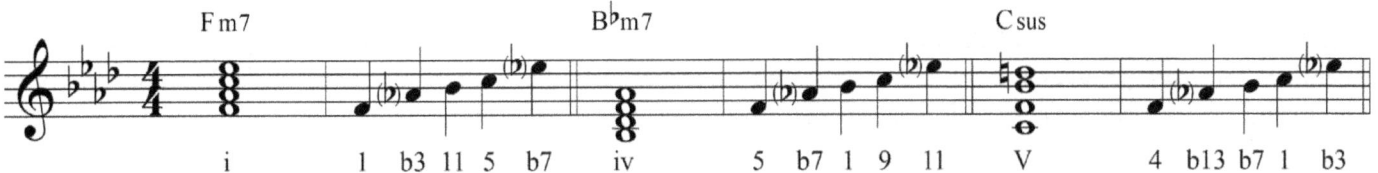

A minor blues can feature straight or swung quavers. This example uses swung quavers, so the stock rhythmic phrases you learned in the first half of Chapter Four will be useful now.

Improvise four-bar question and answer musical sentences over audio Example 7h. The minor blues is a twelve-bar sequence, so three musical sentences make one whole chorus (12 bars).

There are four different versions of this audio track at 90bpm, 120bpm, 150bpm and 180bpm. Start with the slowest and work your way up.

Example 7h:

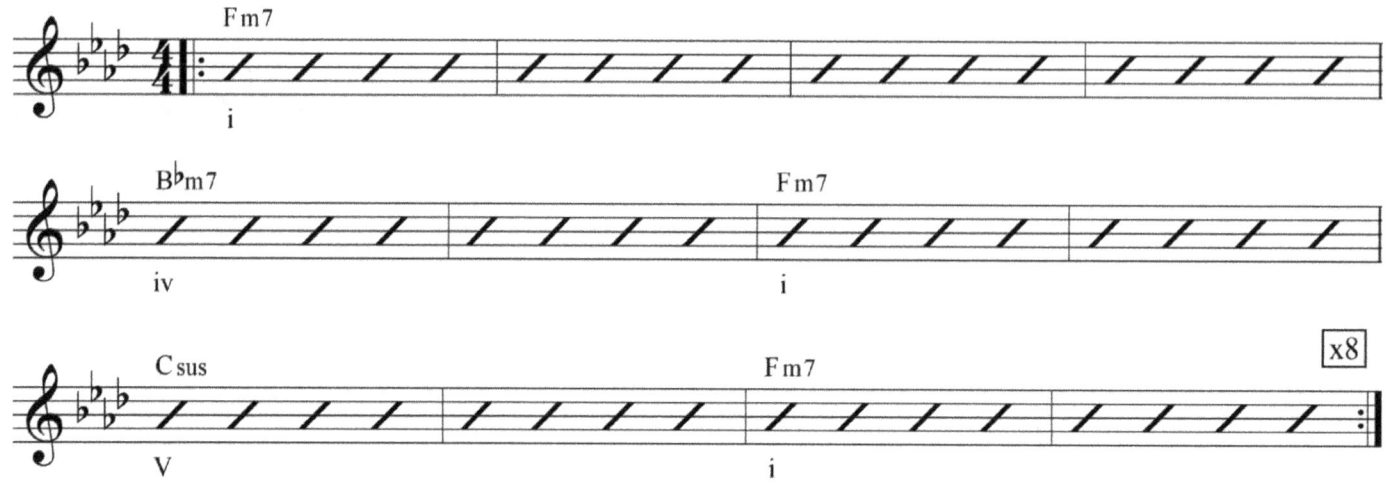

Soloing on a Major Blues

A major blues refers to the regular twelve-bar blues chord progression you are probably familiar with already. This chord sequence is the basis for an entire genre, with all its various styles, which has evolved over the last hundred years.

The major blues is also one of the most common chord sequences used in jazz. However, jazz musicians often disguise this chord progression by substituting and adding chords. They do this to increase the harmonic activity and introduce ii-V sequences, which are more common in jazz tunes.

Sometimes there can be so many chord substitutions, like in *Blues for Alice* by Charlie Parker, that it can look nothing like a blues, but the fundamental underlying structure is the same twelve-bar sequence so we still refer to it as a blues.

Most types of blues music feature guitarists, who use slides and bends to decorate the notes. This sound has become so synonymous with the blues that we are used to hearing these *wrong* notes over the chords and accept them as part of this music. For example, on a blues, it is quite common to play a minor third melody note over a dominant seventh chord, which has a major third. The tension it creates works well in this context and is called a *blue note*. But if you played a major third melody note over a minor chord that would sound very wrong, as it is not something we are used to hearing.

Different styles of music have different protocols, so keeping in context is very important when improvising. It means that what (in theory) is a wrong note, can sound great when used in the right scenario.

Work Song by Nat Adderley is an excellent example of a tune where the melody and soloing are based on a blues scale (minor pentatonic plus #4) but the harmony underneath is all dominant 7th chords. In this context, the minor third in the melody over the major third in the chord works great and gives a strong flavour of the blues. Technically, *Work Song* isn't a blues, it is a sixteen bar *question and answer* song, but it has such a strong flavour of the blues it is referred to as a *sixteen bar blues*.

There are several choices of scale you can use over a major blues, but if you use the *tonic* minor pentatonic scale (F Minor Pentatonic over F Blues), then each note of the scale works with each chord as follows.

Example 7i:

You may notice in the previous example there is one note for each chord that doesn't sound too good (shown in brackets). This is referred to as an *avoid* note. The eleventh (fourth) degree of the scale clashes with the major third of the dominant seventh chord because it creates an interval of a minor ninth (semi-tone), which is a very dissonant interval. However, an *avoid* note does not mean you can't play it. You can use it as a passing note within a phrase but try to avoid playing it on the first beat of the bar, or using it as a long note held over the chord. For now, try not to feature it in your melodic phrase.

A major blues can feature straight or swung quavers. This example uses swung quavers, so the stock rhythmic phrases you learned in the first half of Chapter Four will be useful now.

Improvise four-bar question and answer musical sentences over audio Example 7j. The major blues is a twelve-bar sequence, so three musical sentences make one whole chorus (twelve bars).

There are four different versions of this audio track at 90bpm, 120bpm, 150bpm and 180bpm. Start with the slowest and work your way up.

Example 7j:

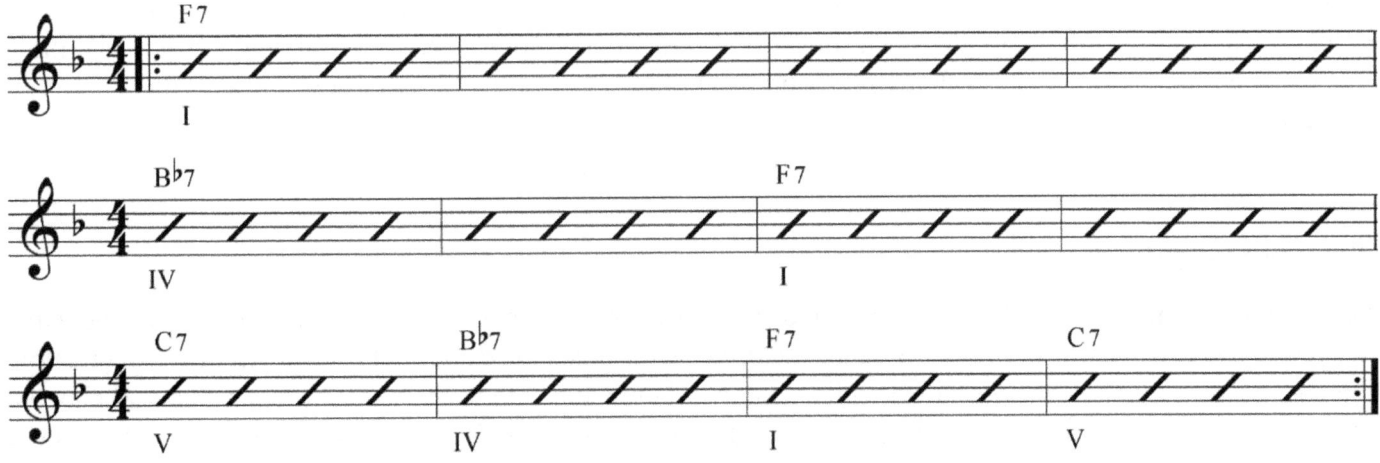

It will take time to develop fluency, but by now you should be feeling confident with improvising in a variety of different styles using straight and swung quavers. You should be hearing most of your question and answer phrases as you play them and not be getting lost in the sequence, which is a real achievement and something you can build on.

So far you have focused on *what* to play. In the next chapter, you are going to focus on *how* to play.

Chapter Eight – Jazz Articulation

Articulation refers to *how* you play each note. Changing the articulation of various notes in a phrase will affect the sound and feel of the whole musical phrase.

Certain jazz musicians tend to favour certain types of articulation, which become part of their individual, recognisable sound, just as different people speak with different accents or dialects. However, some articulation techniques are generic to most jazz musicians and these are a good place to start when trying to develop an authentic jazz sound, particularly with swung quavers.

Notation is limited and unable to express the nuances of subtle performance techniques and timing. You have to have the sound in your head of what it is to *swing,* so ultimately, you can only learn to *swing* by listening to lots of great jazz recordings. You need that point of reference of what it sounds like to *really swing*. But you have to know what to listen for and once these techniques are pointed out, and you have spent some time working on them, you will start to notice them more on recordings.

Articulation markings are often seen in big band parts, but rarely seen in notation for small groups or in *real books*. It is also rare to see articulation markings in transcriptions, where they would be particularly useful. But in all of these scenarios, it is assumed that you will listen to the recordings to learn the articulations.

You have two options when there are no articulation markings on your part. Either, listen to the original recording to find out what the articulation should be, or make up your own articulation using your judgement, which is dependent on you having good taste. You develop good taste by listening to lots of great jazz recordings. So, either way, you have to listen to lots of great jazz recordings!

First, we need to understand some standard musical terminology that is used to define the various articulation techniques. Then you will practise some exercises to help develop these techniques and learn how to play in keeping with the standard jazz protocol. Then you will apply these articulations to some four-bar questions and answer phrases.

There is not space in this book to get into much detail with individual instrumental techniques and it is assumed you know how to play these on your instrument, or if not, can ask your teacher or find demonstrations online. The emphasis here is on thinking about the sound you produce and being aware of how it affects the music you create.

Staccato *vs* Legato

Score markings are usually written in Italian, and this translates to Short vs Long. Staccato and legato affect what happens at the end of each note, which is called the *decay* of the note. Staccato is notated with a dot above or below the note head, and Legato is notated with a line above or below the note head. Staccato means that you play the note short, whatever its rhythmic value. Legato means you hold the note for its full rhythmic value. You can use varying degrees of staccato or legato according to the stylistic requirements of the music at that moment.

Example 8a:

There is no hard and fast rule for applying staccato and legato in jazz and you should experiment with different variations to see how it affects the phrase. Usually, most of the notes in a phrase will be played legato, with one or two notes staccato. When playing swing, if the phrase ends on an up-beat then it would most likely be played staccato.

In the next example, hear how the application of staccato and legato articulations affect the sound of this four-bar phrase played with swung quavers.

Example 8b:

In the next example hear how the application of staccato and legato articulations affect the sound of this four-bar phrase played with straight quavers.

Example 8c:

Now create some of your own four-bar phrases and apply various staccato and legato articulation. Do this in a conscious, deliberate way and determine what articulation you are going to use *before* you play the phrase. Try singing the phrase before you play it, to clarify the articulation in your mind. Prescribing the articulation will help you develop control over your playing.

When you can consistently apply the various articulations that you prescribed, then repeat the improvisation exercises in Chapter Seven and play phrases with the articulation included. Try to hear the phrase, including the articulation, as you play it. Make sure what comes out of the instrument matches what is in your head.

Slurred *vs* Bowed

Slurring and bowing affect what happens at the front of each note, which is called the *attack* of the note.

The speed of the bow movement, the downward pressure on the string and the force with which the bow strikes the string all combine to affect the *attack* of each note. There are many options available and you can use combinations of bowing techniques to emphasise the attack of the note more or less, according to the stylistic requirements of the music at that moment.

Slurring the notes on a violin requires you to play a continuous bowing action whilst fingering different notes with your left hand.

You cannot slur two adjacent notes. The result would be a *tie*, where the two notes are joined together to create one long note.

Slurs are notated with a curved line. If there is no curved line, then the note should be bowed. The first note of a slurred phrase is bowed.

Example 8d:

When playing jazz, it is standard protocol to emphasise the upbeats, usually with a combination of accents and bowing. We'll look at accents in the next section, so for now, let's focus on the bowing.

When playing quaver notes you should bow the upbeats and slur the downbeats. If the phrase starts on a downbeat, then play that first note bowed, then bow the next upbeat and continue alternating slurred and bowed notes. Listen to the audio track to hear how it should sound.

This next example demonstrates this common jazz bowing pattern applied to an F Major scale.

Example 8e:

This bowing pattern places more emphasis on the upbeats and less emphasis on the downbeats, which gives the rhythm more forward motion. It helps it *swing*.

When playing triplets the first note is bowed with the rest slurred, unless preceded by an upbeat quaver, which should be bowed and then the whole triplet would be slurred.

Example 8f:

These bowing patterns are just guidelines, and there are many examples of jazz musicians playing other bowing patterns which also sound great. Practising these exercises will help you develop good habits and give your melodic phrases a more authentic jazz feel.

In the next example hear how the application of bowing and slurring affects the sound of this four-bar phrase played with swung quavers.

Example 8g:

In the next example hear how the application of bowing and slurring affects the sound of this four-bar phrase played with straight quavers.

Example 8h:

As before, create some of your own four-bar phrases and apply the above slurring and bowing guidelines. Do this in a conscious, deliberate way and determine what articulation you are going to use *before* you play the phrase. Again, sing the phrase before you play it to clarify the articulation in your mind. Prescribing the articulation will help you develop control over your playing.

When you can consistently apply the various articulations you prescribed, then repeat the improvisation exercises in Chapter Seven and play phrases with the articulation included. Try to hear the phrase, including the articulation, as you play it. Make sure what comes out of the instrument matches what is in your head.

Accented *vs* Ghosted

Accenting and ghosting affect the volume of an individual note, unlike dynamic markings, which change the volume of a whole phrase or section of music.

There are two different types of accent used in jazz articulation. > over a note means play it louder and for its full length. ^ over a note means play it louder and short.

But the question is *how* loud? Dynamics are always relative, and accents are not always *ff*. A general guideline is to play one dynamic marking louder than is marked for the rest of the phrase. If you are playing *pp* then your accented note should be *p*, but this is only a guideline, and ultimately it is down to your judgement as to what sounds right for the music at that particular moment.

Ghost notes are indicated by placing brackets around the note. Ghosting a note means playing it very quietly so that it is barely perceptible. The effect should be to hint at the note rather than explicitly play it.

Using combinations of accents and ghost notes can bring a musical phrase to life. This technique is called *shading*. One analogy is to think of a great Shakespearean actor reciting lines in a play at the Globe Theatre *vs* a year three child reciting lines in a school nativity play. One can bring the story to life and grab the attention of the audience with their delivery, while the other can leave the audience repeatedly looking at their watch. I'll let you decide which is which!

As mentioned before, when playing jazz, it is standard protocol to emphasise the upbeats, so a good exercise is to practise accenting every upbeat and ghosting every downbeat. When practising you should play slowly and exaggerate this technique by overemphasising the accents. In performance, and as you increase speed, the accents should be lighter and subtler.

This next example demonstrates accents and ghost notes applied to an F Major scale.

Example 8i:

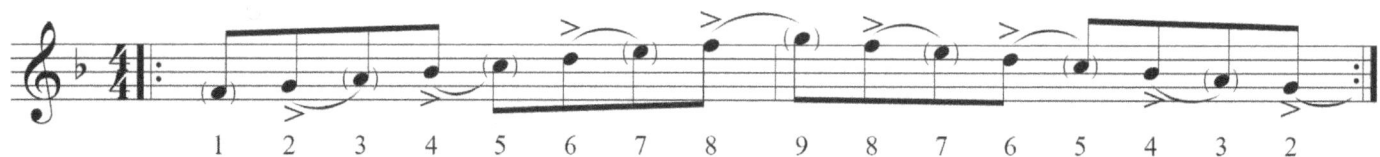

The previous example is an excellent exercise to develop the technique, but you should vary the accents and ghost notes when performing and use accents on some downbeats as well. Use your judgement and apply them at suitable moments to help bring your musical phrase to life.

In the next example hear how the application of accents and ghost notes affect the sound of this four-bar phrase played with swung quavers.

Example 8j:

In the next example hear how the application of accents and ghost notes affect the sound of this four-bar phrase played with straight quavers.

Example 8k:

Once again, create some of your own four-bar phrases and apply the above accent and ghost note articulations. Do this in a conscious, deliberate way and determine what articulation you are going to use *before* you play the phrase. Again, sing the phrase before you play it to clarify the articulation in your mind. Prescribing the articulation and sticking to it will help you develop control over your playing.

When you can consistently apply the various articulations that you prescribed, then repeat the improvisation exercises in Chapter Seven and play phrases with the articulation included. Try to hear the phrase, including the articulation, as you play it. Make sure what comes out of the instrument matches what is in your head.

Putting It All Together

You have learned several articulation techniques to help bring your musical phrases to life and give your playing a more authentic jazz sound. Now you are going to put them all together.

Applying this level of detail to a phrase is challenging because it requires a lot of control over your instrument, so don't worry if you can't play these exercises perfectly on the first go. Take your time. They are meant to be something for you to work on rather than play straight through.

Listen to the audio files several times *before* you attempt each exercise. Make sure you have the sound of the phrase, with the correct articulation, in your head before you try to play it. If necessary, break down each phrase into smaller sections, work on the sections separately, then join them back together.

Work on one phrase at a time until you get it. Then try some different articulations on that phrase and see how many different ways you can play it using all of the various articulation techniques.

In the next example, hear how the application of various articulations affect the sound of this four-bar phrase played with swung quavers.

Example 8l:

In the next example hear how the application of various articulations affect the sound of this four-bar phrase played with straight quavers.

Example 8m:

At first, it will require a considerable amount of thought and conscious effort to play all of the articulations accurately. With practice, you will gain fluency, and this procedure will become more automated. The articulations will embed into your improvising and become something that you process on a subconscious level, in *real time*, as you play.

Having spent some time working on articulation you will start to notice these details on the recordings by your favourite jazz artists.

Finally, repeat the improvisation exercises in Chapter Seven and play your own melodic phrases with your own articulations included. Try to hear the phrase, with all its articulations, in your head as you play it. Remember what you learned back in Chapter One.

Hear What You Play And Play What You Hear

Other Techniques

You have worked on the most common articulation techniques, but there are some other effects that you need to know about.

Vibrato

Vibrato is the effect of raising and lowering the pitch of a sustained note. This is achieved on the violin by *rolling* the left fingers over the strings. The range of pitch alteration can be wide or narrow. The vibrato can be fast or slow, and it can also change speed. Using vibrato is a way of making your instrument sound more like a human voice and enables you to be more expressive. It can be particularly effective on ballads, where long notes are common, but is used less on faster tunes. Classically trained musicians tend to use a lot of vibrato, which can be a difficult habit to break when playing jazz. Early jazz musicians tended to play with a very pronounced vibrato, but it was used much less from the be-bop era onwards.

Listen to Stuff Smith and Stéphane Grappelli duetting on *How High The Moon* from *Stuff and Steff* and hear how Smith uses a very pronounced, wide vibrato at the start of many of his phrases to create energy. Grappelli also uses vibrato, but not so often and when he does it is lighter and more *classical* in feel.

Listen to Joe Venuti's early recording of *Apple Blossoms* with Eddie Lang and hear how he uses a lot of vibrato throughout his playing. Compare this to Jean-Luc Ponty's recording of *Au Privave* on his 1964 debut album, where he uses virtually no vibrato, searching for a be-bop sound on the violin.

All of them sound great and demonstrate how the different use of vibrato can affect a performance and become an identifiable part of a musician's individual style.

Glissando and Portamento

Sometimes referred to as *sliding up* to a note, glissando is another effect that was more popular in early styles of jazz and is used less in modern jazz. It involves starting a note under pitch then sliding the note up to its true pitch, or it can be used to connect two melody notes. A glissando can also move downwards. Some instruments, like trombone and timpani, have a built-in ability to glissando over a wide range, whereas other instruments, like piano, cannot play a true glissando but instead play a chromatic scale between the notes. Portamento is a subtler variation of glissando which involves changing the fingering mid-way, giving a partial glissando.

Listen to Ray Nance's beautiful 1969 recording of *Take The A Train,* with Roland Hannah on piano, where he uses glissando and portamento with great taste.

Double Stopping and Pizzicato

On violin it is possible to play two notes at the same time using various combinations of open strings and/or fingerings. This technique is called *double stopping.* Listen to Leroy Jenkins on his tribute to Albert Ayler from his 1978 album *The Legend of Ai Glatson.* He uses double stopping to create a polyphonic phrase on the main theme of this piece.

Pizzicato is the technique of plucking the string with the fingers instead of bowing. This can be used by either hand in combination with bowing and other effects. Check out Mark Feldman's incredibly intense recording *Smoke* from his 1999 album with Sylvie Courvoisier *Music for Violin and Piano* where he uses a combination of pizzicato and various bowing techniques.

Developing an Individual Sound

Timbre

And lastly, timbre (*tone*) is one of the most distinctive elements of a musician's sound and a very personal choice.

Check out Stuff Smith *vs* Stéphane Grappelli, or Ray Nance *vs* Jean-Luc Ponty, or Joe Venuti *vs* Leroy Jenkins. They are all violinists, all with very contrasting tones, all of which sound great.

All of these musicians have an identifiable sound. To a certain degree, the style of music they played affected them, but these artists had such a strong musical identity that they and their sound ultimately transformed the music they played.

The bright, singing quality and effortlessness of Stéphane Grappelli's violin combined with Django Reinhardt's hard-swinging guitar was what made their recordings so successful. The energy, rhythm and full sound of Jean-Luc Ponty's solo on *Armando's Rhumba,* from Chick Corea's 1976 album *My Spanish Heart,* is what makes that recording so great. Ray Nance's sweet tone and sublimely beautiful phrasing on the 1958 studio recording of Duke Ellington's *Black, Brown & Beige* goes a long way to making that album the classic it is.

The point is, it wasn't just a violin on *Minor Swing*, it was Stéphane Grappelli. It wasn't just a violin on *Armando's Rhumba*, it was Jean-Luc Ponty. It wasn't just a violin on *Black, Brown & Beige*, it was Ray Nance. The individual sound of those musicians had such an impact on those recordings it made them the masterpieces they were. And surely this is the pinnacle of any artistic endeavour.

In the early stages, it can be confusing to know who, or what you want to sound like. They are all great! One approach is to pick an artist you like the sound of and focus on them for a while. Get hold of as many of their recordings as you can and listen to them every day. Completely immerse yourself in their playing. Try to copy their sound and articulation as much as possible. After a few months move on to another artist you like and do the same. After you have done this with four or five different artists, you will have the foundations for your own sound to emerge, which will be a combination of all of those great ingredients.

Chapter Nine – Composition

Composing is like improvising, but with the benefit of hindsight to edit your ideas. Unlike improvising, you can change anything you are not happy with. You have the luxury of time to go back and tweak your raw ideas and shape them in to well-balanced melodies.

Question and answer phrases are such a familiar feature in all styles of music they work great as a basis for almost any type of composition. To demonstrate this concept, I have written four tunes in different styles and forms, all using the same method you have learned in this book. I simply created question and answer phrases with the same minor pentatonic scale and put them in different musical contexts. You could have written any of these tunes!

Sample Jazz Blues Composition - Sunny Honeymoon

This tune is a *riff* blues, which is a particular type of jazz or blues tune, and was inspired by the Sonny Rollins composition *Sonnymoon for Two*. A riff blues uses a single four-bar phrase and repeats it over a twelve-bar blues chord progression. This example uses the descending minor pentatonic scale with a question and answer structure.

A riff blues is something that can be composed on the spot and would often feature in big band swing groups like the Count Basie Band. They had to play long evenings of music and keep people dancing, so they would make up new melodies as they performed and sometimes these new tunes became a fixture in the set.

There are several riff blues tunes that have become part of the classic jazz repertoire. Check out the following examples: *C Jam Blues, Centerpiece, Bag's Groove, Night Train, Blues In The Closet, Chitlins con Carne,* and of course *Sonnymoon For Two*.

Play the head (main theme) twice, then improvise for three choruses (three x twelve bars), then play the head twice again to finish. It is standard protocol to play the head of a twelve-bar blues twice.

Example 9a:

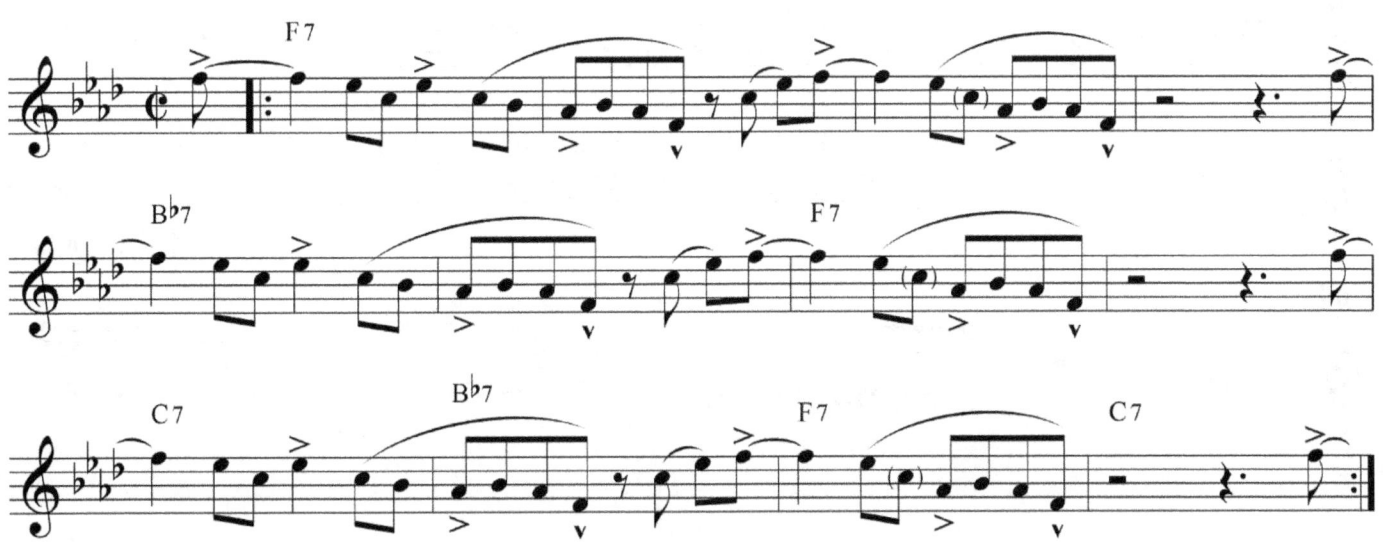

Sample Funky Composition - Funky Fourteen

This tune uses the same minor pentatonic scale over a funky, straight eighth rhythm section groove. It features two question and answer phrases with a tag to complete the melody. The structure is a minor blues with an extra two bars at the end, making it a fourteen-bar blues. Those extra two bars just felt right to me in the overall shape of the music. Be careful not to lose your place in the solo sequence. As well as counting, listen out for the drum fills, which are used to mark important structural points in the chord sequence.

Play the tune twice, then improvise for two choruses, then play the tune twice again. On the last chorus the final tag of the melody is played four times, with the last two up an octave.

Example 9b:

Sample Latin Composition – Major General Mambo

This tune uses the same minor pentatonic scale you have learned, but the harmonic sequence is based on the relative major key (Ab). Using a major key signature gives the tune a more up-beat feel, which fits the style. All of the notes in the minor pentatonic work fine over these chords, but try resolving your phrases on Ab now, instead of the F, and you will hear that this is the new *home* key. This is the same concept that you learned on the pop groove in Chapter Seven.

The structure of this tune is ABA with each section lasting for eight bars, which means the whole tune is twenty-four bars long. Play the head once, then improvise for three choruses (three x ABA), then play the last head once. Again, listen out for the drum fills during the solo sequence to help you keep the structure. On the last chorus jump to the fifth time bar to play the ending.

Example 9c:

Sample 12/8 Blues Composition – Hot Tea, Shall I Put It There

This tune is in the style of a classic rhythm and blues 12/8 and was inspired by my wife bringing me a cup of tea! Notice the familiar *tutti* (everyone playing in unison) figure in the rhythm section at the start of each phrase. The tune works as an answer phrase to the *tutti* question in the rhythm section.

Again, play the head twice, then improvise for three choruses (three x twelve bars) then play the head twice to finish.

Example 9d:

How To Compose Your Own Tune

Now you are going to compose your own *riff* blues, like the first example in this chapter.

You have already improvised lots of question and answer phrases, so using one of them to create your own twelve bar riff blues is going to be easy. Just remember the steps you have learned:

- Don't resolve the question phrase (don't end on 1)
- Do resolve the answer phrase (do end on 1)
- Make the question and answer belong together by using a similar rhythm for both phrases

Start by improvising a few four-bar musical sentences, like you did in Chapter Six. Pick one you like the sound of. Play it a few times. Try a few different variations with the rhythm until you settle on a version which feels most natural. You have a composition!

Now try it over the rhythm section backing track. Play the head twice (six musical sentences), improvise for three choruses then play the head twice again to finish.

Example 9e:

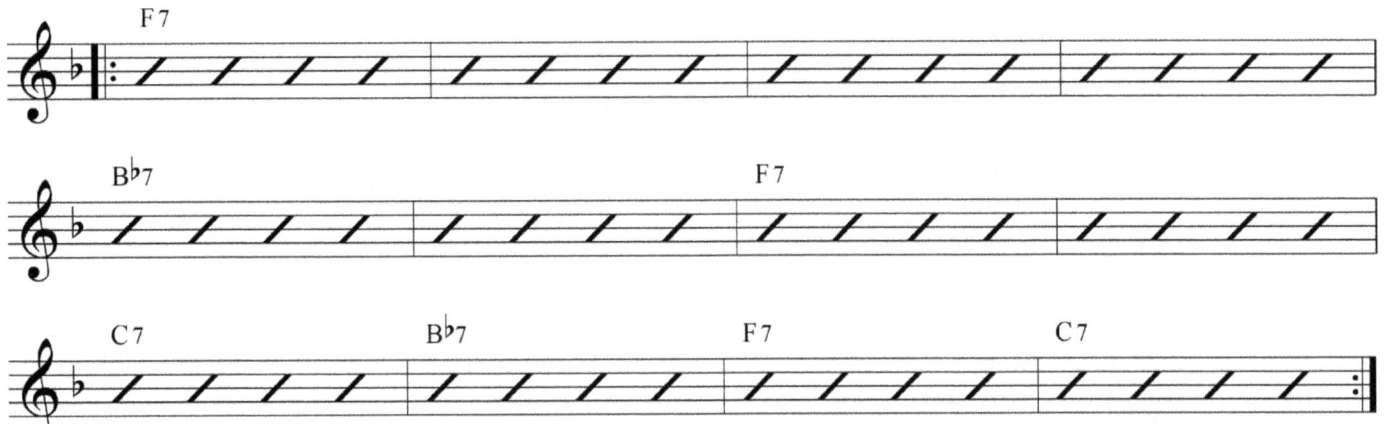

Chapter Ten – Taking it Further

Using Minor Pentatonics over a ii-V-I

ii-V-I refers to a short sequence of diatonic chords from the major scale that features extensively throughout the standard jazz repertoire. This chord sequence is so common, often showing up more than once in the same tune, that it is essential for all students of jazz to have an understanding of ii-V-I's. There is a lot of material published about the ii-V-I, and there are many different approaches to improvising over it, which you should also check out.

One advantage of the minor pentatonic scale is its ability to fit over several different chords. Because there are only five notes in the scale it has a certain vagueness about its harmonic implications, which means you can play the same minor pentatonic scale over all three chords in the ii-V-I sequence. Freeing yourself from thinking too much about the underlying harmony means you can focus on creating good melodic phrases and developing your motivic ideas through the chord sequence.

However, the harmonic vagueness of the pentatonic scale is also its weakness. Using the same pentatonic scale over a series of chords means you won't be hitting the strong, functional notes of each chord in the sequence (the thirds and sevenths). Your improvised solo won't be clearly outlining the harmony and, as they say, you won't be "making the changes".

This is a matter of aesthetics and stylistic choice. Improvising with a minor pentatonic scale will give your solo a particular sound and feel and, like anything, if you only use one sound it will eventually become tiresome to the listener. The great improvisers all used a range of different techniques and concepts in their solos, and you should aim to do the same. But for now, using the minor pentatonic is a great way to start soloing over ii-V-I sequences and something you can build on.

Wrong notes and *avoid* notes

A highly skilled and experienced jazz musician can make any note sound good on any chord, depending on how they approach and depart that note. It is merely a matter of some notes sounding more dissonant than others. These are sometimes referred to as "tension notes" or *playing outside* the harmony. But it takes a lot of skill and experience to pull this off and not sound like you are playing wrong notes.

When you are starting out you need to learn to play *inside* the harmony, which means playing notes that fit the underlying harmonic sequence. Using chord tones for your solo, or notes from the scale which are implied by the particular chord or chord progression will mean you are playing *inside*.

As mentioned in Chapter Seven, there are some notes in a scale which sound tense when played over certain chords. Even though they are, technically, the right notes they do not sit well on the chord and should not be featured. These are referred to as *avoid* notes. You can play these notes as passing notes within a phrase, but you should avoid playing them on the first beat of the bar or holding them over a chord.

One example of an avoid note is the fourth degree of a major scale played over a major chord. Try it and you will hear the tension it creates with the major third in the chord. The fourth (or eleventh) degree of the major scale gives an interval of a semi-tone (or minor ninth) against the major third, which is a very dissonant interval. It is not a *wrong* note, but you wouldn't want to feature it.

Using a scale with no *avoid* notes makes life much easier because you don't have to worry about this problem. If you play the minor pentatonic scale built on the major third of the key signature (the I chord) you can play it over the whole ii-V-I sequence and will have no *wrong* notes or *avoid* notes to deal with.

Now let's look at why.

If you play a ii-V-I chord sequence in Db major you get the following chords.

Example 10a:

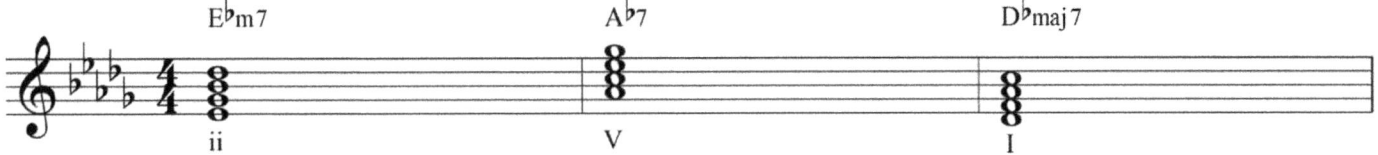

All of the chords are diatonic to Db Major, which means they only use notes from the Db Major scale. There are no other notes from outside the scale.

The major third of Db Major is F. If you play an F Minor Pentatonic scale over all three chords of the ii-V-I sequence in Db Major you will have no *wrong* notes or *avoid* notes to deal with. The following three examples explain why.

Chord ii

Chord ii in the key of Db is Ebm7, and the notes of this chord are Eb, Gb, Bb, Db. If you play F Minor Pentatonic (F, Ab, Bb, C, Eb) over Ebm7 you are playing the 9, 11, 5, 13 and 1 of this chord. None of these are *wrong* notes or *avoid* notes. They all work fine and do not clash with the chord, but you are not hitting the b3 or b7, which are the main functional notes. So F Minor Pentatonic works OK over an Ebm7 chord, but it is not a particularly strong sound.

Example 10b:

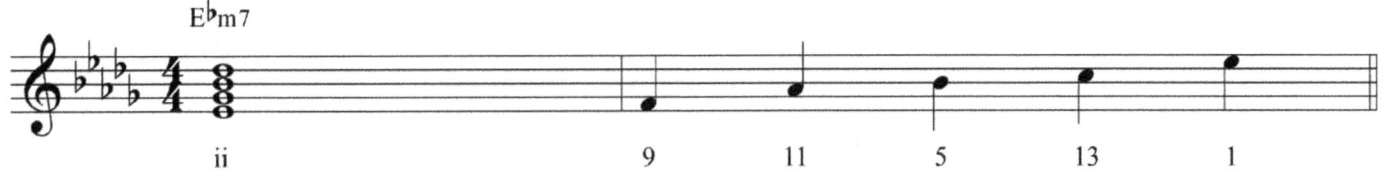

Chord V

Chord V in the key of Db is Ab7, and the notes of this chord are Ab, C, Eb, Gb. If you play F Minor Pentatonic (F, Ab, Bb, C, Eb) over Ab7 you are playing the 13, 1, 9, 3 and 5 of this chord. Again, there are no *wrong* notes or *avoid* notes and this time you are hitting the 3, which is a strong choice. So F Minor Pentatonic works well over an Ab7.

Example 10c:

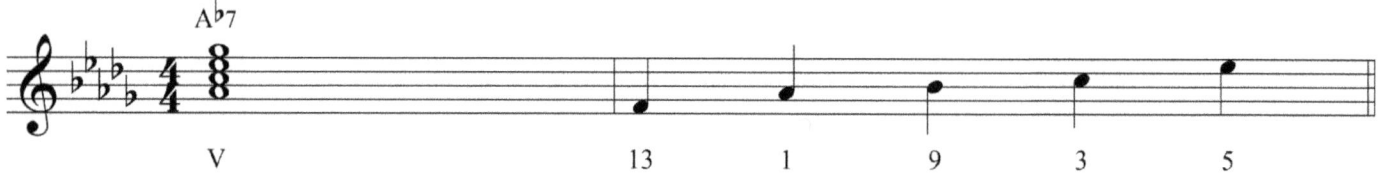

Chord I

Chord I in the key of Db is Dbmaj7, and the notes of this chord are Db, F, Ab, C. If you play F Minor Pentatonic (F, Ab, Bb, C, Eb) over Dbmaj7 you are playing the 3, 5, 13, 7, 9 of this chord. Again, there are no *wrong* notes or *avoid* notes and this time you are hitting the 3 and the 7, so F Minor Pentatonic works very well over Dbmaj7.

Example 10d:

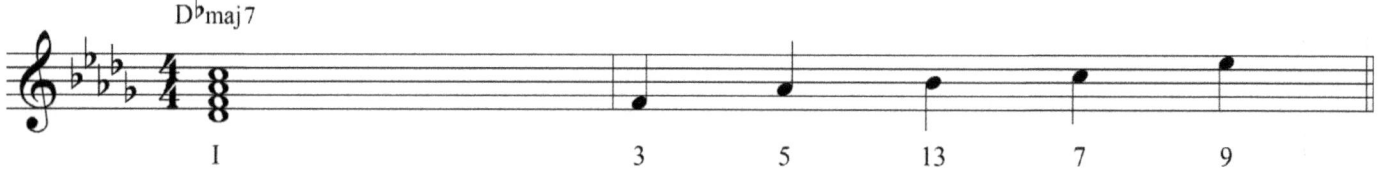

Now you are going to put all that theory into practice and improvise over a ii-V-I chord sequence in the key of Db Major using the F Minor Pentatonic scale. This exercise uses a four-bar vamp and the backing tracks are recorded at various speeds. Start with the slowest speed and work your way up.

Example 10e:

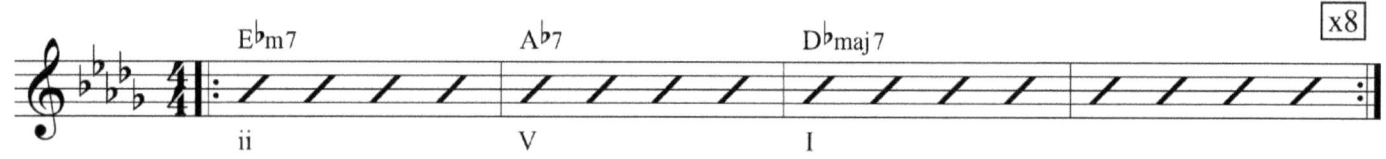

Working In Other Keys

Everything you have learned in this book has used an F Minor Pentatonic scale. You have learned everything in one key, but there are twelve different keys. Ideally, you should practise everything in all twelve keys. But, you don't have to do it all at once. Learning everything in all keys is a massive undertaking and a long-term goal.

To start with, take what you have learned and transpose it to one or two other familiar keys. Gradually, with practice, you will become more fluent at transposing your scales and melodies into different keys.

Using numbers instead of letters to identify each note is helpful when transposing because the numbers don't change, but the letters do. Of course, you need to know what the notes are (the letters), but if you think in numbers, then everything is the same no matter what the key. Using numbers means you are thinking harmonically, which helps you to understand what you are playing. Once you have transposed the same thing through a few keys, you will appreciate the benefit of using numbers instead of letters.

In the next example you will transpose the F Minor Pentatonic scale to Bb Minor Pentatonic scale. You did this in Chapter Two using the interval sequence, but this time the notation is given. Notice the new key signature has one extra flat.

Example 10f:

When you change the key signature the 1 becomes a different note, but every other note has the same relationship to the 1. Therefore, we can use the same numbers in this new key to define each note of the scale.

If you transpose the first scale pattern exercise you learned in Example 3a into the new key, you get the following (notice that the numbers are the same, but the notes are different):

Example 10g:

There isn't sufficient space in this book to transpose all of the examples through all twelve keys, but hopefully the above demonstration is enough to clarify the concept for you.

This book has covered some essential concepts and techniques required for jazz improvisation, based on methods I use in some of my jazz workshops. I hope you enjoyed developing these skills and your knowledge and confidence has increased to the point where you feel comfortable improvising and creating your own music.

Learning to improvise and play jazz is a lifelong pursuit. It takes a lot of work but can be very rewarding. The more you practice, the more you will improve. The more you study, the more you will understand and appreciate this great art form. You never really *get there*. The secret is to get the most out of the journey.

You can reach me through my website **www.busterbirch.co.uk**

Best wishes and thank you.

Buster

www.ingramcontent.com/pod-product-compliance
Lightning Source LLC
LaVergne TN
LVHW061256060426
835507LV00020B/2335